WELCOME TO THE U.S.A.
WISCONSIN

Written by Ann Heinrichs   Illustrated by Matt Kania
Content Adviser: Brett Barker, PhD, Assistant Professor
of History, University of Wisconsin-Marathon County,
Wausau, Wisconsin

The Child's World

J 917.75
Heinrichs

Published in the United States of America by The Child's World®
PO Box 326 • Chanhassen, MN 55317-0326
800-599-READ • www.childsworld.com

Photo Credits
Cover: Timothy Hursley/Milwaukee Art Museum; frontispiece: Wisconsin
Department of Tourism.

Interior: Corbis: 10 (Richard Cummins), 15 (Richard Hamilton Smith), 31
(Bettmann); Experimental Aircraft Association: 35; Getty Images: 20 (Jamie
Squire/Allsport), 22 (Time Life Pictures/Keri Pickett), 26 (Stone/Zane Williams),
30 (Jonathan Daniel); The House on the Rock: 32; Library of Congress: 24; Prairie
du Chien Area Chamber of Commerce: 6; Summerfest: 17; Ray Thornborough: 38;
Wisconsin Department of Tourism: 9, 13 (R. J. & Linda Miller), 18, 25, 28.

Acknowledgments
The Child's World®: Mary Berendes, Publishing Director

Editorial Directions, Inc.: E. Russell Primm, Editorial Director; Katie Marsico, Associate
Editor; Judith Shiffer, Assistant Editor; Matt Messbarger, Editorial Assistant; Susan
Hindman, Copy Editor; Melissa McDaniel, Proofreader; Peter Garnham, Matt
Messbarger, Olivia Nellums, Chris Simms, Molly Symmonds, Katherine Trickle, Carl
Stephen Wender, Fact Checkers; Tim Griffin/IndexServ, Indexer; Cian Loughlin O'Day,
Photo Researcher and Editor

The Design Lab: Kathleen Petelinsek, Design and art production

Library of Congress Cataloging-in-Publication Data
Heinrichs, Ann.
  Wisconsin / written by Ann Heinrichs ; cartography and illustrations by Matt Kania.
    p. cm. — (Welcome to the U.S.A.)
  Includes index.
  ISBN 1-59296-288-2 (lib. bdg. : alk. paper) 1. Wisconsin—Juvenile literature.
2. Wisconsin—Geography—Juvenile literature. I. Kania, Matt. II. Title. III. Series.
  F581.3.H453 2005
  977.5—dc22   2004005715

Ann Heinrichs is the author of more than 100 books for children and young adults. She has also enjoyed successful careers as a children's book editor and an advertising copywriter. Ann grew up in Fort Smith, Arkansas, and lives in Chicago, Illinois.

About the Author
Ann Heinrichs

Matt Kania loves maps and, as a kid, dreamed of making them. In school he studied geography and cartography, and today he makes maps for a living. Matt's favorite thing about drawing maps is learning about the places they represent. Many of the maps he has created can be found in books, magazines, videos, Web sites, and public places.

About the
Map Illustrator
Matt Kania

On the cover: **The Milwaukee Art Museum is located along the shores of Lake Michigan.**
On page one: **The Kewaunee Pier stretches into Lake Michigan.**

OUR WISCONSIN TRIP

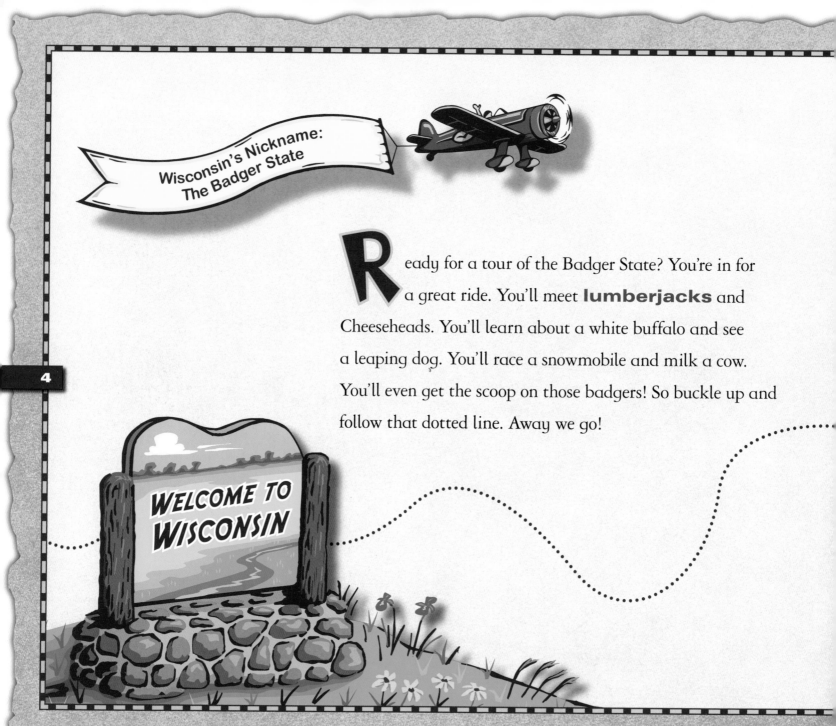

Wisconsin's Nickname:
The Badger State

4

Ready for a tour of the Badger State? You're in for a great ride. You'll meet **lumberjacks** and Cheeseheads. You'll learn about a white buffalo and see a leaping dog. You'll race a snowmobile and milk a cow. You'll even get the scoop on those badgers! So buckle up and follow that dotted line. Away we go!

WELCOME TO WISCONSIN

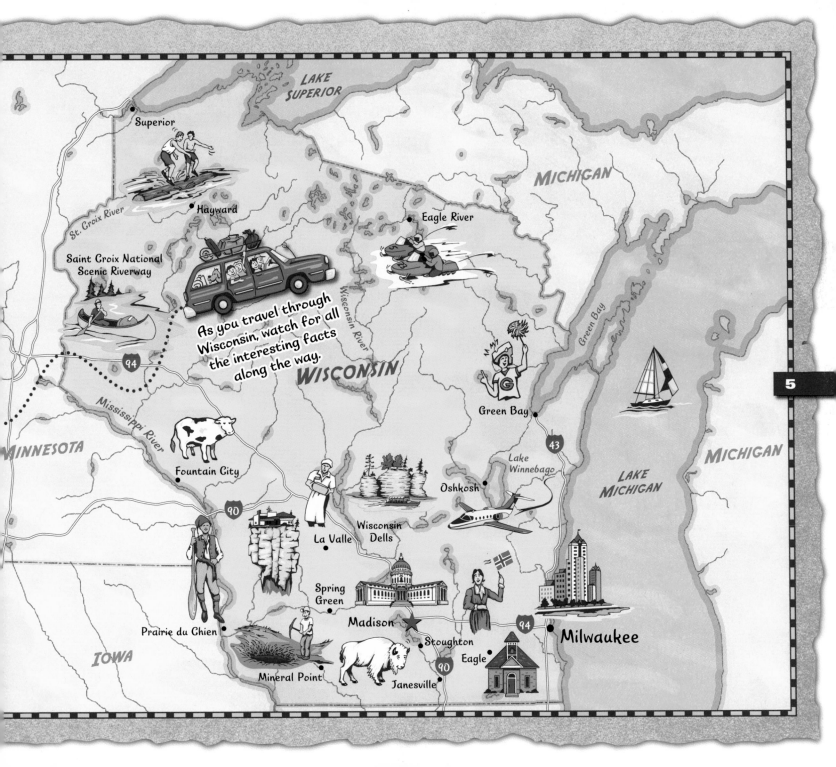

LAKE SUPERIOR

Superior

Hayward

St. Croix River

Saint Croix National Scenic Riverway

MINNESOTA

Mississippi River

Fountain City

Prairie du Chien

IOWA

Mineral Point

La Valle

Wisconsin Dells

Spring Green

Madison

Stoughton

Janesville

Eagle

MICHIGAN

Eagle River

Wisconsin River

WISCONSIN

As you travel through Wisconsin, watch for all the interesting facts along the way.

Green Bay

Oshkosh

Lake Winnebago

Milwaukee

Green Bay

LAKE MICHIGAN

MICHIGAN

Would you have been a good fur trader? Find out at Prairie Villa Rendezvous!

The Madeline Island Historical Museum is in La Pointe. This island was an Ojibwe and French fur-trading center.

Whap! The whip snaps, cutting a potato in two. Chunk! The **tomahawk** chops into a stump. You're at the Prairie Villa Rendezvous! Prairie du Chien holds this event every year. It celebrates life in Wisconsin's early days.

Frenchmen were the first Europeans in Wisconsin. Jean Nicolet was the first to arrive. He was a French explorer from Canada. Nicolet arrived in Green Bay in 1634. He claimed Wisconsin for France. Soon other Frenchmen arrived. They traded with Native Americans for furs.

Prairie du Chien was a fur-trading post in the 1700s. Native Americans and French traders met there. They exchanged goods and shared customs and skills.

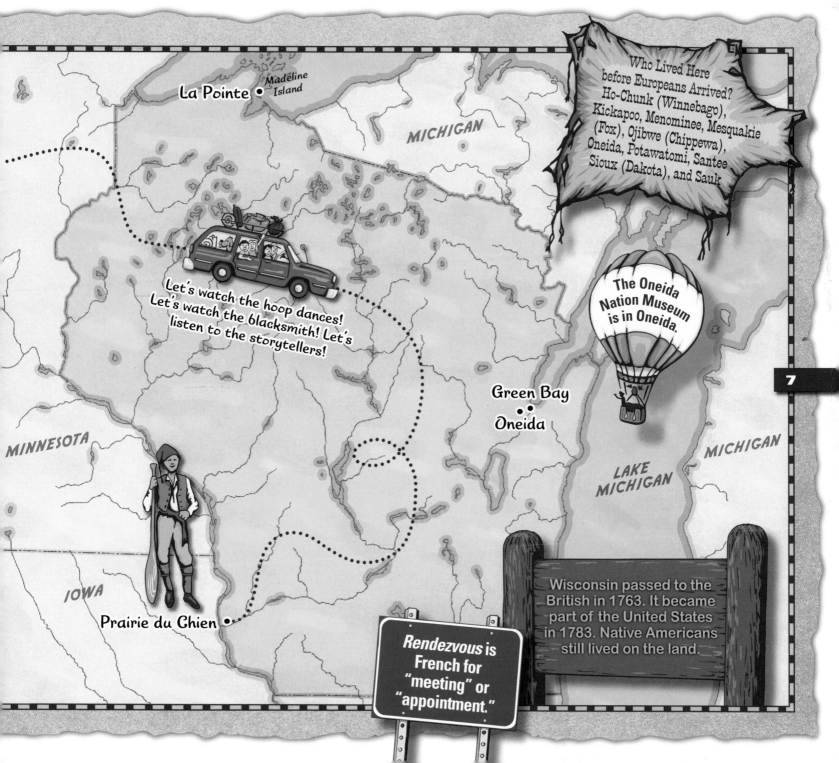

La Pointe

Madeline Island

MICHIGAN

Who Lived Here before Europeans Arrived? Ho-Chunk (Winnebago), Kickapoo, Menominee, Mesquakie (Fox), Ojibwe (Chippewa), Oneida, Potawatomi, Santee Sioux (Dakota), and Sauk

Let's watch the hoop dances! Let's watch the blacksmith! Let's listen to the storytellers!

The Oneida Nation Museum is in Oneida.

Green Bay
Oneida

MINNESOTA

MICHIGAN

LAKE MICHIGAN

IOWA

Prairie du Chien

Rendezvous is French for "meeting" or "appointment."

Wisconsin passed to the British in 1763. It became part of the United States in 1783. Native Americans still lived on the land.

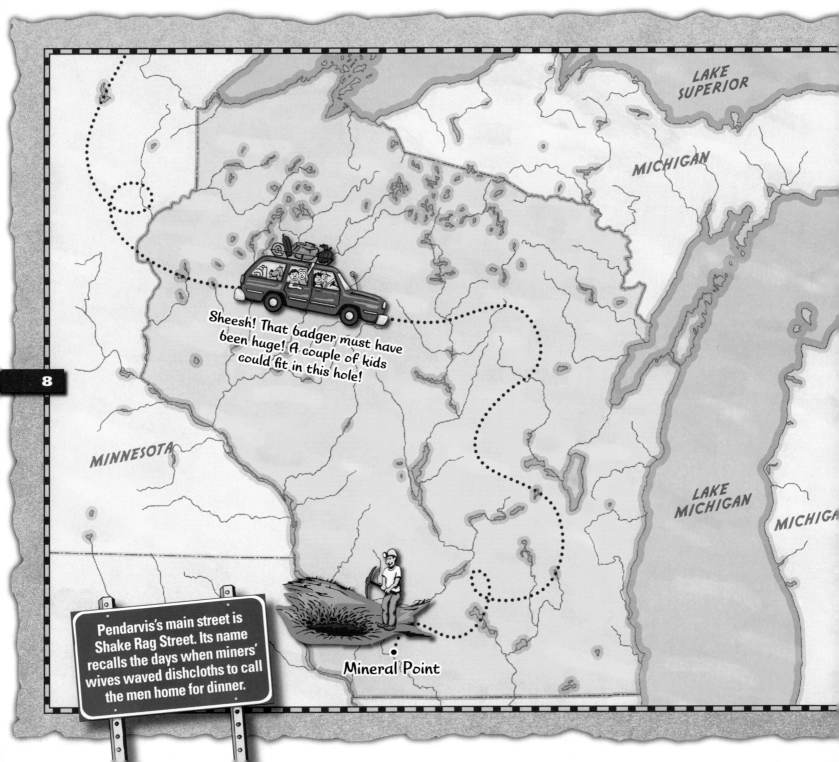

Badger Holes in Mineral Point

Roam the hills around Pendarvis. You'll see big holes here and there. What are those holes all about?

Pendarvis is an old miners' village in Mineral Point. Lead was discovered there in the 1820s. Thousands of **immigrants** came in to work the mines.

At first, the miners had no houses. They lived in holes they dug in the hillsides. People called these shelters badger holes. That's why Wisconsin is called the Badger State!

Residents of Pendarvis eventually built houses instead of badger holes.

Pendarvis was settled by Cornish miners. They came from Cornwall in England.

Badgers have thick bodies and large front claws. They dig complex underground tunnels.

And you thought you had chores! An actor carts hay at Old World Wisconsin.

Wisconsin was the 30th state to enter the Union. It joined on May 29, 1848.

Old World Wisconsin near Eagle

There's a woman wearing a long dress. She's boiling potatoes over an open fire. Beyond the log cabin, a man is plowing. A horse pulls his wooden plow. What are these folks up to? Just ask!

You're at Old World Wisconsin near Eagle. It's like an 1800s immigrant village. People in native clothing are busy at their chores. They'll tell you exactly what they're up to!

People from many lands moved into Wisconsin. Some came from Denmark, Finland, or Norway. Others came from Germany, Poland, Ireland, or Wales. African Americans came, too. Everyone worked hard to make new homes.

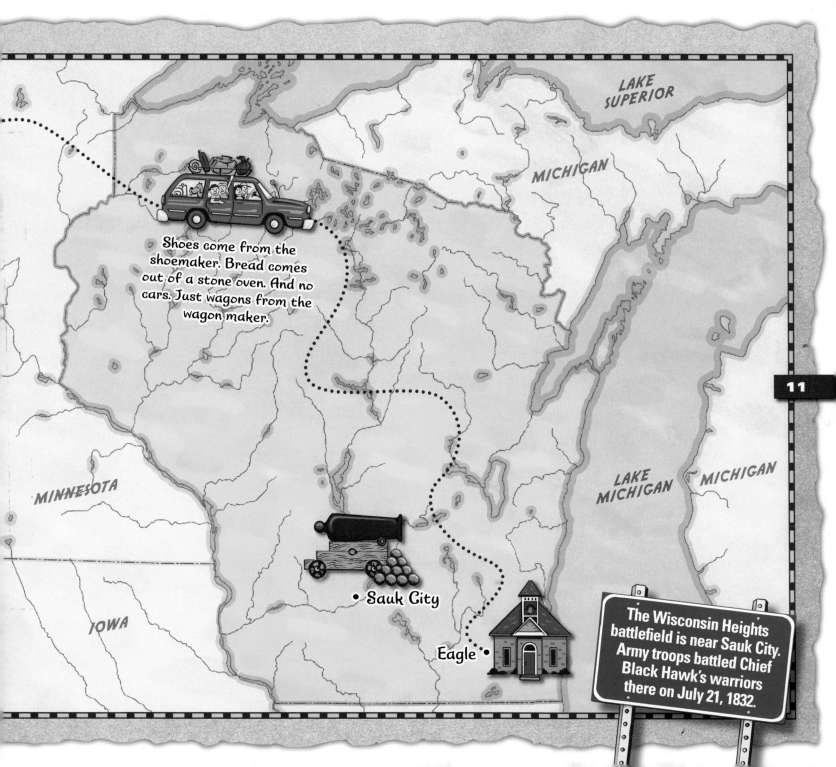

Shoes come from the shoemaker. Bread comes out of a stone oven. And no cars. Just wagons from the wagon maker.

LAKE SUPERIOR

MICHIGAN

MINNESOTA

LAKE MICHIGAN   MICHIGAN

IOWA

• Sauk City

Eagle •

The Wisconsin Heights battlefield is near Sauk City. Army troops battled Chief Black Hawk's warriors there on July 21, 1832.

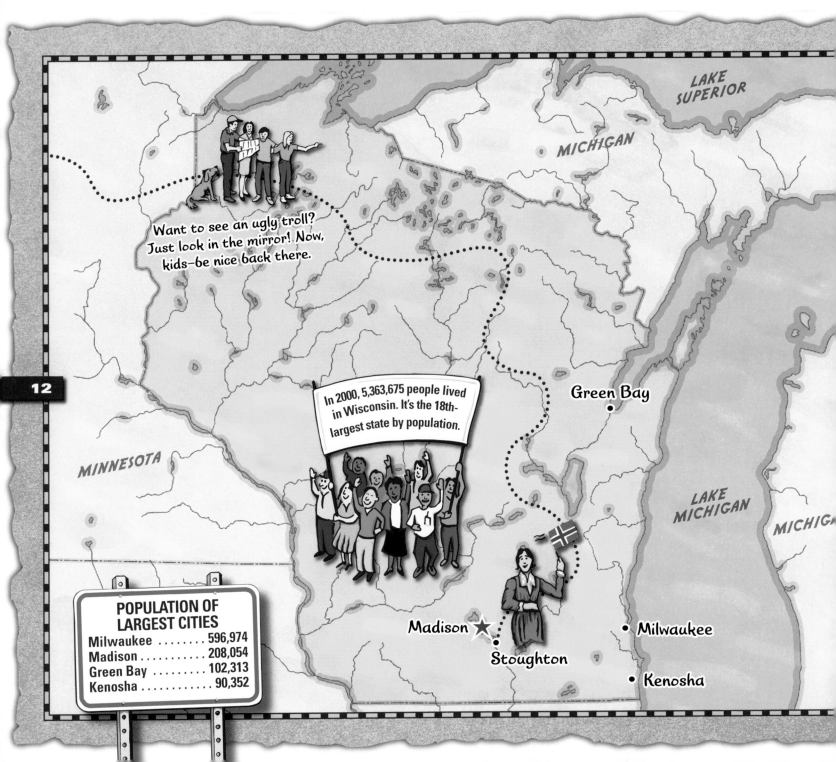

Want to see an ugly troll? Just look in the mirror! Now, kids—be nice back there.

LAKE SUPERIOR

MICHIGAN

In 2000, 5,363,675 people lived in Wisconsin. It's the 18th-largest state by population.

Green Bay

MINNESOTA

LAKE MICHIGAN

MICHIGAN

Madison ★

Stoughton

• Milwaukee

• Kenosha

POPULATION OF LARGEST CITIES
Milwaukee 596,974
Madison 208,054
Green Bay 102,313
Kenosha 90,352

Syttende Mai in Stoughton

Draw an ugly **troll**. Make it look really mean and snarling. Maybe you'll win the ugly-troll-drawing contest! It's part of Syttende Mai. That's a big Norwegian festival in Stoughton.

Wisconsin's **ethnic** groups hold lots of fun festivals. For Germans, it's Oktoberfest. Czechs hold Cesky Den. Asians celebrate the Moon Festival. Polish, Italian, Mexican, French—you name it! They all share their food, music, and fun.

Wisconsin residents march in an Oktoberfest parade.

Yo-ho! That's lumberjack talk for "Hello!"

Are you fast on your feet? Maybe you should try log rolling!

14

Look around. Sawdust and wood chips are flying. People are wobbling on logs in the water. Oops—somebody fell in!

You're at the Lumberjack World Championships in Hayward. It celebrates Wisconsin's logging days. Logging was a big **industry** in the late 1800s.

Dense forests once covered northern Wisconsin. Lumberjacks cut the trees down. They floated the logs down the rivers. The logs went to sawmills and paper mills.

By the way, lumberjacking is not an all-male sport. Women and girls compete, too. They're called lumberjills!

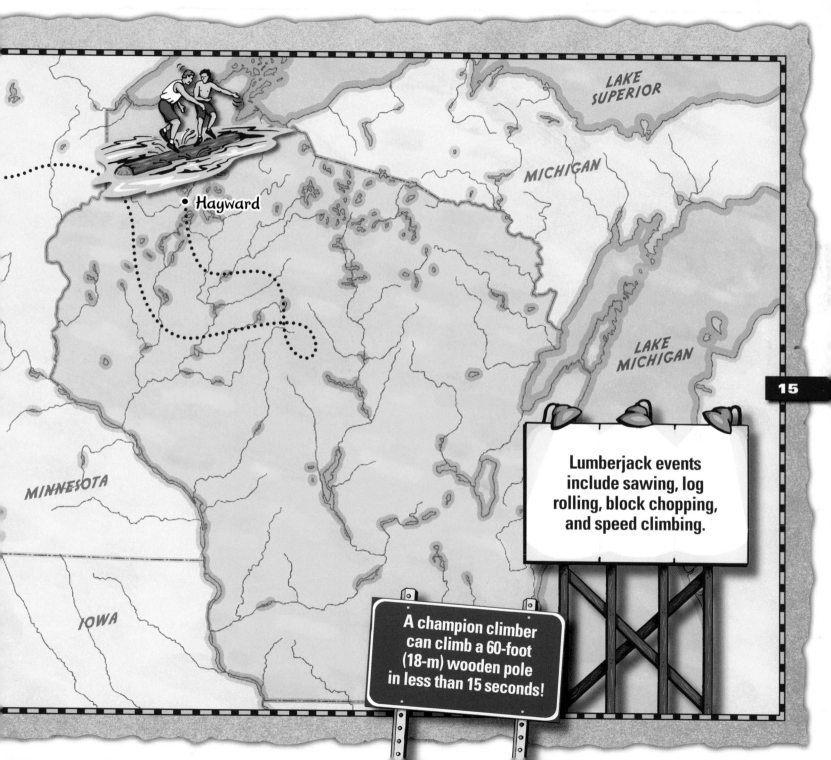

LAKE SUPERIOR

MICHIGAN

LAKE MICHIGAN

• Hayward

MINNESOTA

IOWA

Lumberjack events include sawing, log rolling, block chopping, and speed climbing.

A champion climber can climb a 60-foot (18-m) wooden pole in less than 15 seconds!

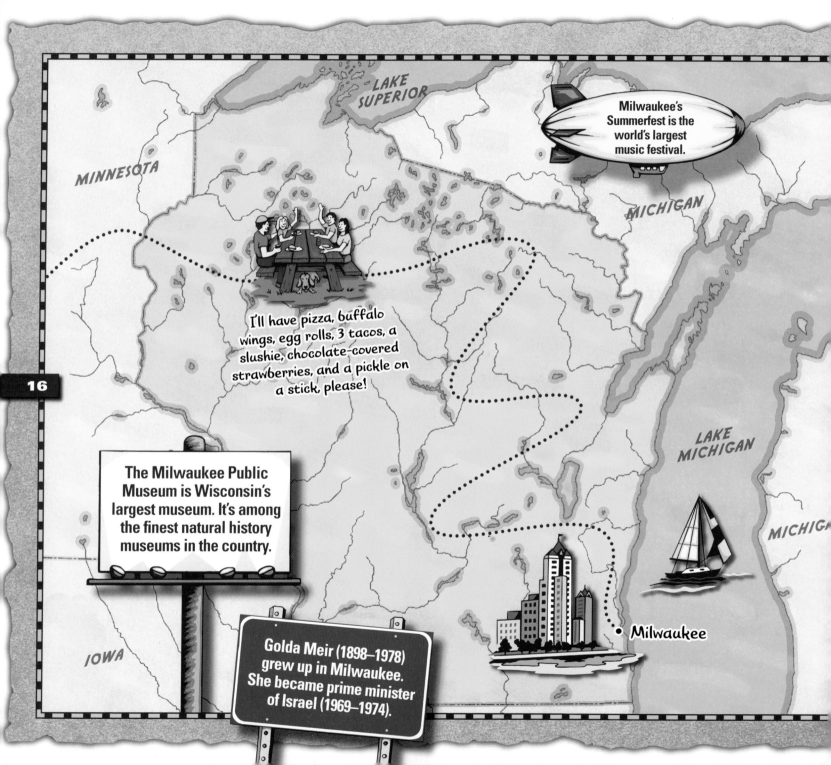

Summerfest in Milwaukee

If you're hungry, head to Summerfest. This visitor is enjoying fried cheese curds.

Hundreds of musicians. Jillions of food stands. It's Summerfest time in Milwaukee!

Thousands of people visit Milwaukee for Summerfest. But Milwaukee works as hard as it plays. It's booming with business and industry.

Many immigrants settled in Milwaukee. They helped the city grow. They worked in flour mills and meat plants. German people opened beer **breweries.** Ships and railroads shipped their goods out. Milwaukee became a center for both manufacturing and banking. Now it's the biggest city in Wisconsin.

You mean "dells" like the Farmer in the Dell? Nope—that dell is a valley. These dells are cliffs.

Wisconsin Dells and the Leaping Dog

He crouches. He springs. He sails through mid-air. Good doggie! This is no circus— it's the Wisconsin Dells. Rushing waters carved its towering rock formations. You'll see the dog at Stand Rock. He leaps across to it from a high cliff. Give that dog a treat!

The Dells are in south-central Wisconsin. High cliffs rise in the southwest, too. Rolling plains cover much of central Wisconsin. The north is hilly with many little lakes.

Wisconsin borders two of the Great Lakes. Lake Superior is on the north. Lake Michigan is on the southeast. Now, think of Wisconsin as a mitten. The Door **Peninsula** would be its thumb!

Pack your suntan lotion and your lifejacket! It's time to sail on Lake Superior.

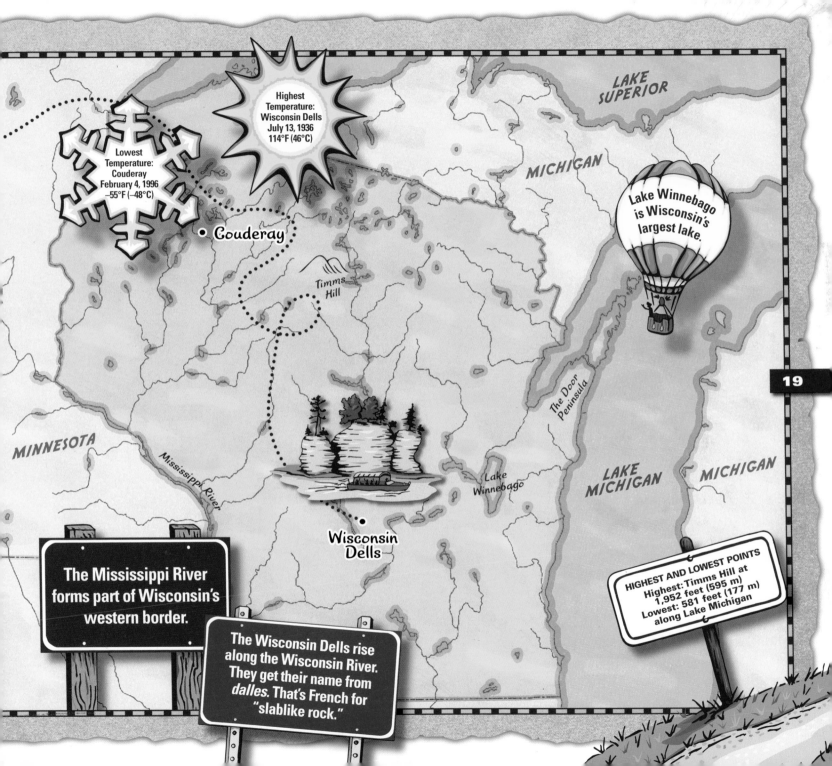

Lowest Temperature: Couderay February 4, 1996 −55°F (−48°C)

Highest Temperature: Wisconsin Dells July 13, 1936 114°F (46°C)

Lake Winnebago is Wisconsin's largest lake.

LAKE SUPERIOR

MICHIGAN

The Door Peninsula

MINNESOTA

Mississippi River

Couderay

Timms Hill

Wisconsin Dells

Lake Winnebago

LAKE MICHIGAN

MICHIGAN

The Mississippi River forms part of Wisconsin's western border.

The Wisconsin Dells rise along the Wisconsin River. They get their name from *dalles.* That's French for "slablike rock."

HIGHEST AND LOWEST POINTS
Highest: Timms Hill at 1,952 feet (595 m)
Lowest: 581 feet (177 m) along Lake Michigan

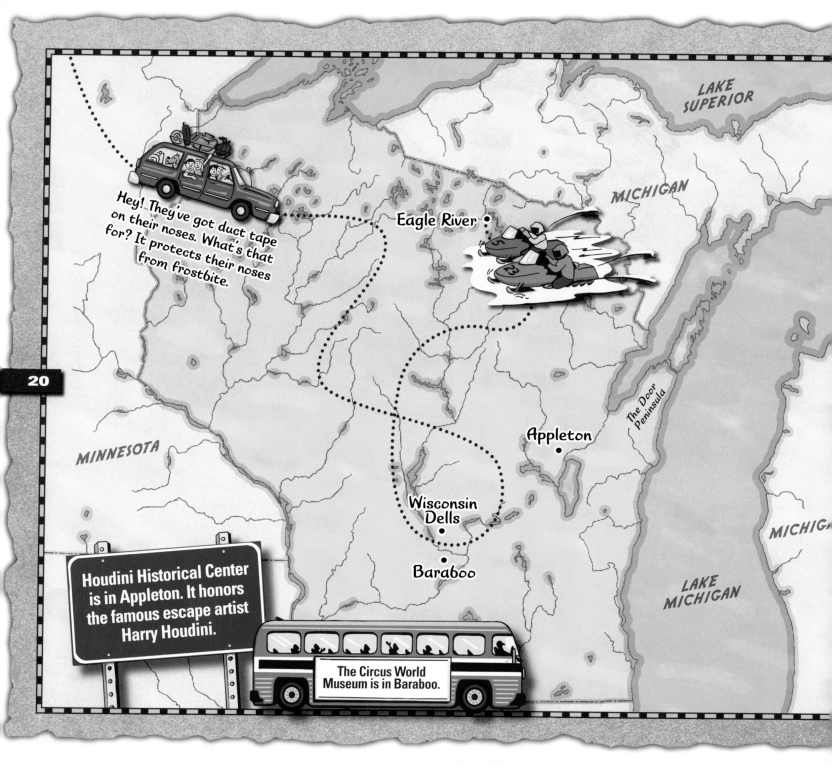

Hey! They've got duct tape on their noses. What's that for? It protects their noses from frostbite.

LAKE SUPERIOR

MICHIGAN

Eagle River

The Door Peninsula

MINNESOTA

Appleton

MICHIGAN

Wisconsin Dells

Baraboo

LAKE MICHIGAN

Houdini Historical Center is in Appleton. It honors the famous escape artist Harry Houdini.

The Circus World Museum is in Baraboo.

The World Championship Snowmobile Derby in Eagle River

Dashing through the snow. In a what? A Ski-doo and an Arctic Cat? No one-horse open sleighs here. You're at the World Championship Snowmobile Derby! Why not join the racers? There's a division for kids, too.

Wisconsin is a great place for winter sports. You can ski, ice-skate, and snowmobile. And sleigh rides? You can get those, too!

For summer fun, there's hiking, biking, and fishing. The Door Peninsula is popular for camping. Wisconsin Dells offers boat rides and water parks. And then there's that leaping dog!

Ladies and gentlemen, start your snowmobiles! The race is on in Eagle River.

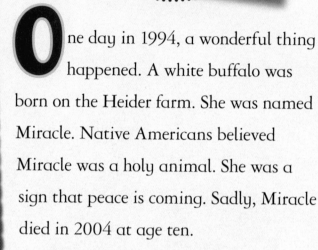

Miracle, the White Buffalo of Janesville

Miracle attracted visitors even as a baby!
Buffalo babies are called calves.

The hodag is Rhinelander's official animal. Hodags are mean and fierce. They have sharp teeth and claws and spikes along their back. But they don't really exist!

One day in 1994, a wonderful thing happened. A white buffalo was born on the Heider farm. She was named Miracle. Native Americans believed Miracle was a holy animal. She was a sign that peace is coming. Sadly, Miracle died in 2004 at age ten.

Buffaloes used to roam across Wisconsin's plains. But hunters killed off the big herds. Many other animals still live in Wisconsin's woods. The thickest forests are in the north. They're home to deer, bears, foxes, and rabbits. And don't forget the badgers! They still dig holes in the hillsides.

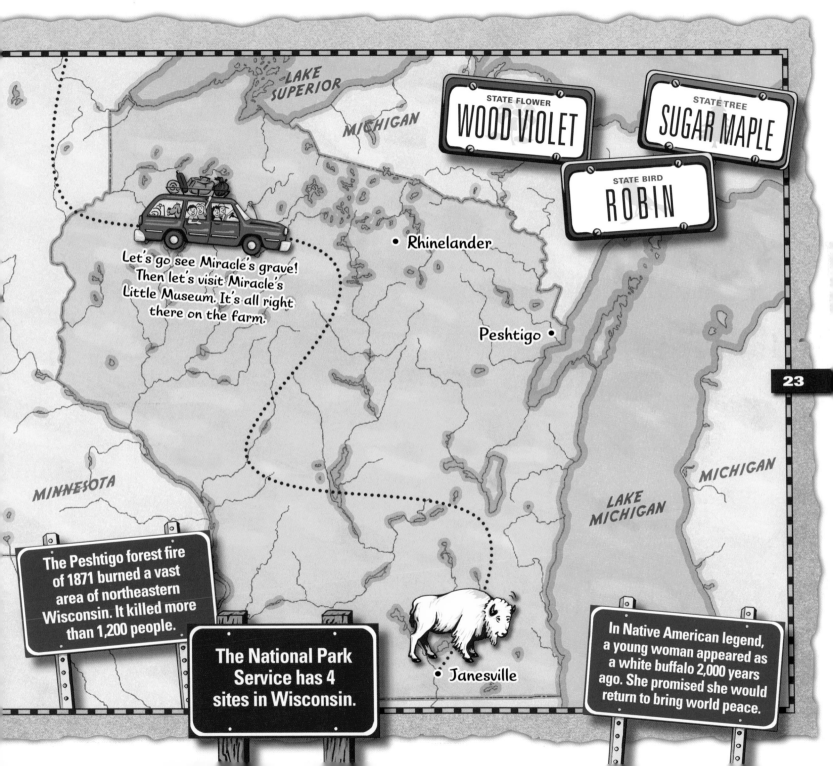

LAKE SUPERIOR

MICHIGAN

STATE FLOWER
WOOD VIOLET

STATE TREE
SUGAR MAPLE

STATE BIRD
ROBIN

• Rhinelander

Peshtigo •

Let's go see Miracle's grave!
Then let's visit Miracle's
Little Museum. It's all right
there on the farm.

MINNESOTA

LAKE MICHIGAN

MICHIGAN

The Peshtigo forest fire
of 1871 burned a vast
area of northeastern
Wisconsin. It killed more
than 1,200 people.

The National Park
Service has 4
sites in Wisconsin.

• Janesville

In Native American legend,
a young woman appeared as
a white buffalo 2,000 years
ago. She promised she would
return to bring world peace.

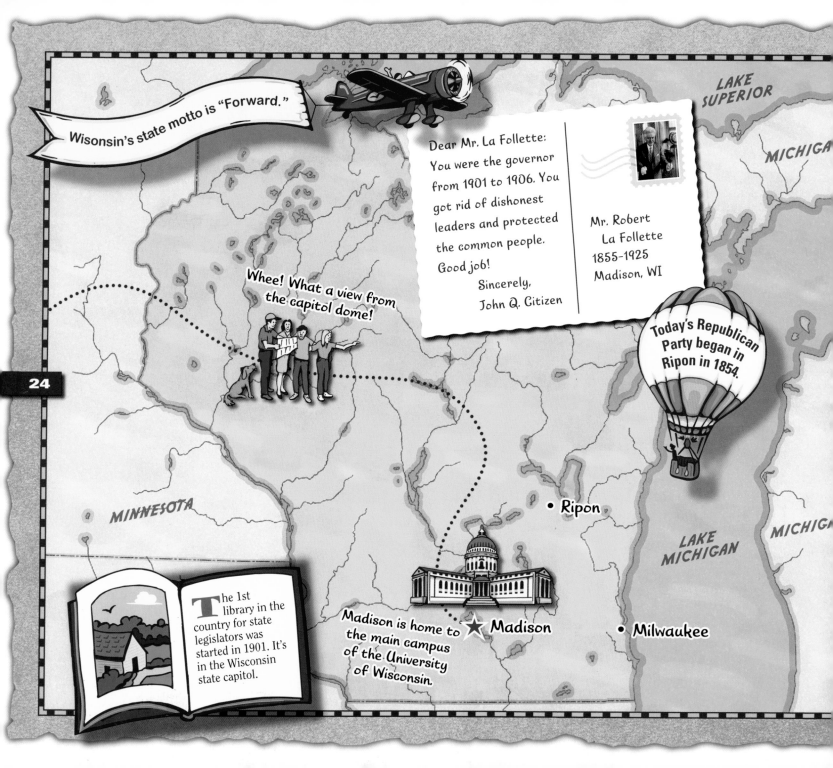

Wisonsin's state motto is "Forward."

Dear Mr. La Follette:
You were the governor
from 1901 to 1906. You
got rid of dishonest
leaders and protected
the common people.
Good job!
Sincerely,
John Q. Citizen

Mr. Robert
La Follette
1855-1925
Madison, WI

Whee! What a view from
the capitol dome!

Today's Republican
Party began in
Ripon in 1854.

LAKE
SUPERIOR

MICHIGAN

MINNESOTA

• Ripon

LAKE
MICHIGAN

MICHIGAN

The 1st
library in the
country for state
legislators was
started in 1901. It's
in the Wisconsin
state capitol.

Madison is home to
the main campus
of the University
of Wisconsin.

★ Madison

• Milwaukee

The State Capitol in Madison

The Wisconsin state capitol dates back to 1917.

Climb up into the state capitol's dome. You feel like you're on top of the world! Look down and see two sparkling lakes. Look out and see Madison's buildings and neighborhoods. And right underneath you are the state government offices.

Wisconsin's government has three branches. One branch is the **legislature.** It makes state laws. The governor leads another branch. It carries out the laws. Courts make up the third branch. Their judges decide whether laws have been broken.

Welcome to Madison, the capital of Wisconsin!

William Rehnquist was born in Milwaukee in 1924. He became chief justice of the U.S. Supreme Court in 1986.

A Dairy Farm Vacation in Fountain City

Baa! Give that calf its bottle! Moo! Time to milk those cows! You call this a vacation? Yes! It's a Room to Roam farm vacation. You're on a **dairy** farm in Fountain City. The guests help with the chores. And they say it's **udder**-ly fantastic!

Wisconsin has thousands of dairy cattle. They give tons of milk! Much of that milk becomes butter and cheese. Lots of farmers raise beef cattle and hogs. Others grow corn, hay, or oats. Many of these crops become animal feed.

Like milk? Then head to a Wisconsin dairy farm!

What Are Wisconsin's Fishing Products?
Whitefish, lake trout, and perch

The Mustard Museum in Mount Horeb has more than 2,300 kinds of mustard.

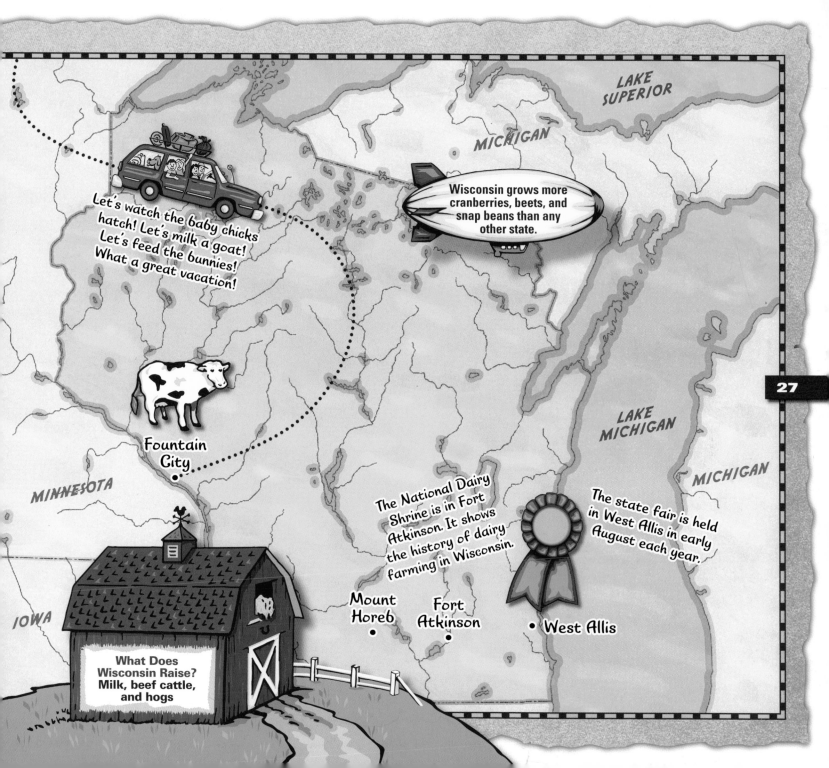

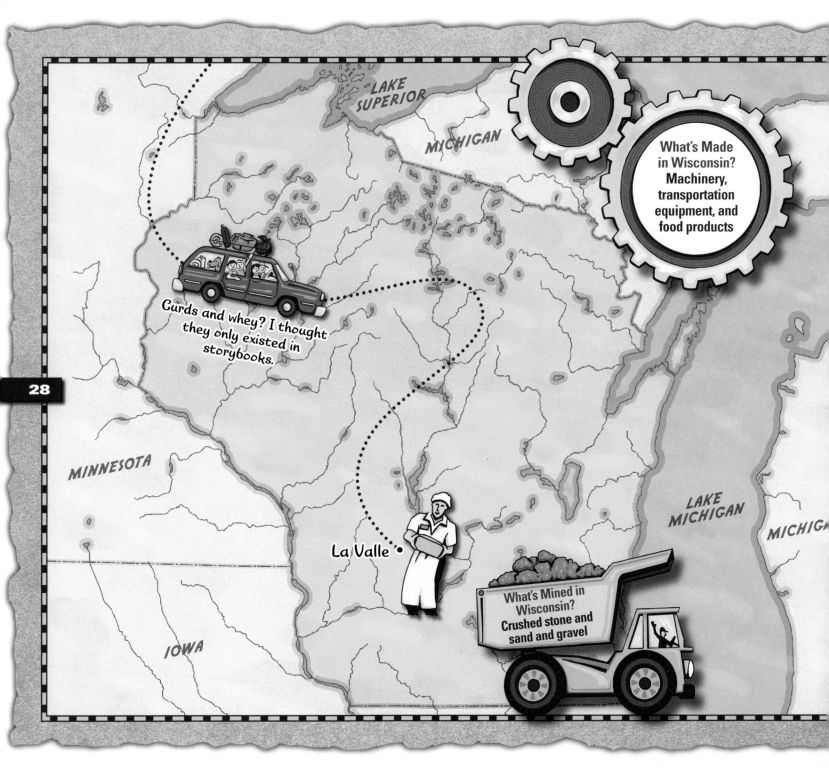

Hot vats of steamy milk. Lumpy curds and creamy whey. Then, at last, the finished product. Golden wheels of cheese! You're touring Carr Valley Cheese factory in La Valle. You see every step of the cheese-making process. Of course, there's a treat at the end. You munch your heart out on free samples!

Got milk? Wisconsin does. Just think of all those cows. Much of their milk ends up as cheese. You'll find cheese factories all over the state.

Wisconsin also makes "hogs"! That's a nickname for motorcycles. Harley-Davidson motorcycles come from Wisconsin. Sorry, no free samples!

Vroom! Riders celebrated the 100th anniversary of Harley-Davidson in 2003.

29

Green Bay's Cheeseheads

Hey, Mom, how about some Cheesehead earrings? How about a Cheesehead soap-on-a-rope?

Grab your Cheesehead hat! It's time to cheer on the Packers!

t looks like cheese. It's shaped like cheese. It's even got holes like Swiss cheese. But don't bite in! It's a Cheesehead hat!

Wisconsin loves its Green Bay Packers football team. Packers fans call themselves Cheeseheads. They wear big cheese-wedge hats. Cheeseheads are loyal fans. They pack Lambeau Field season after season.

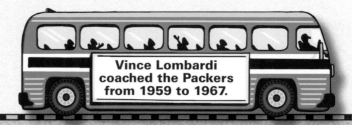

Vince Lombardi coached the Packers from 1959 to 1967.

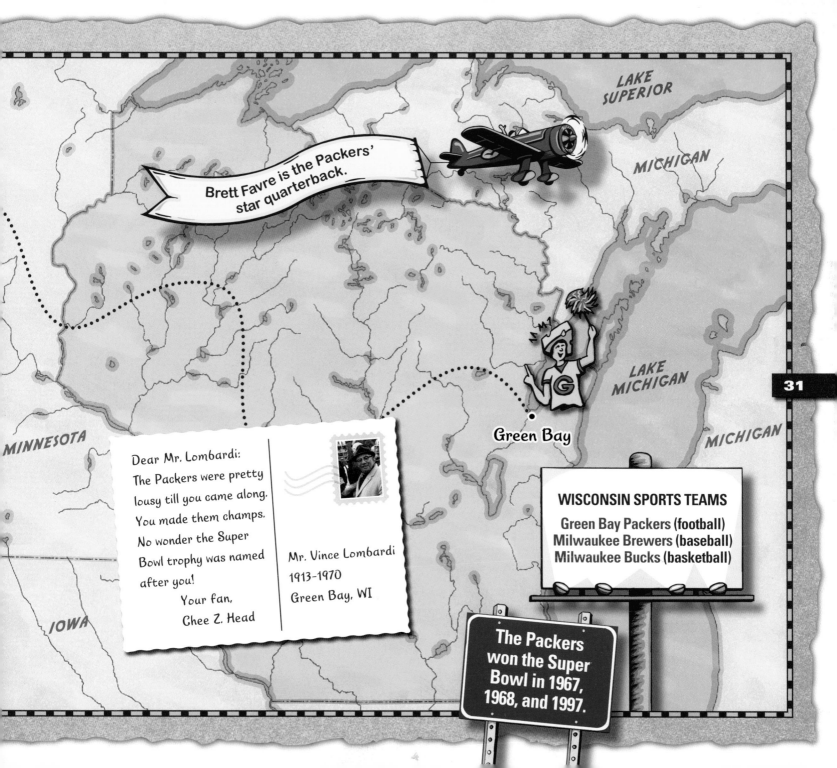

Brett Favre is the Packers' star quarterback.

LAKE SUPERIOR

MICHIGAN

LAKE MICHIGAN

MICHIGAN

Green Bay

MINNESOTA

IOWA

Dear Mr. Lombardi:
The Packers were pretty
lousy till you came along.
You made them champs.
No wonder the Super
Bowl trophy was named
after you!
            Your fan,
            Chee Z. Head

Mr. Vince Lombardi
1913-1970
Green Bay, WI

WISCONSIN SPORTS TEAMS
Green Bay Packers (football)
Milwaukee Brewers (baseball)
Milwaukee Bucks (basketball)

The Packers
won the Super
Bowl in 1967,
1968, and 1997.

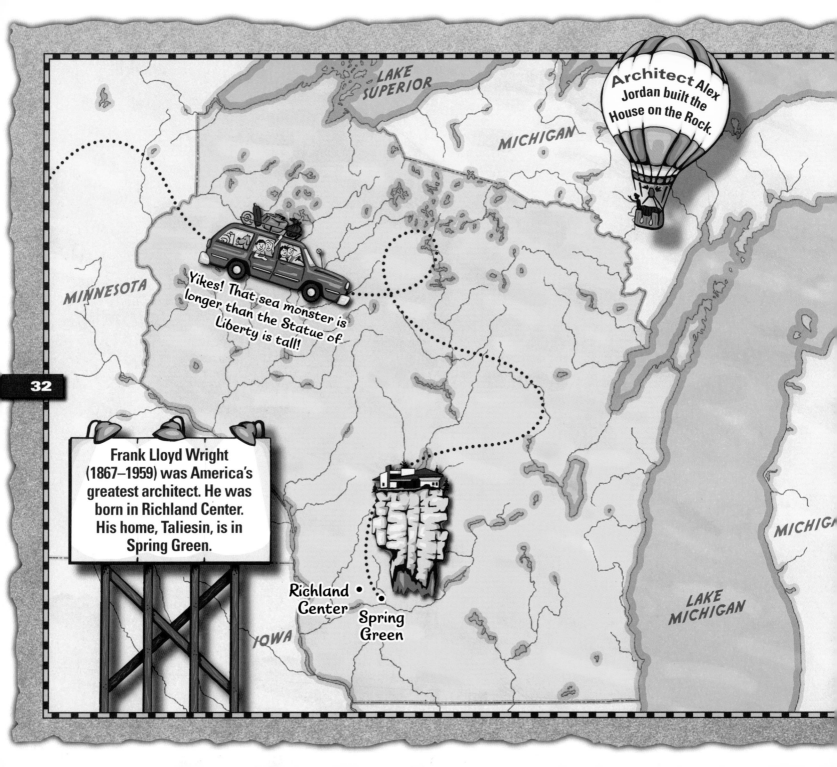

Architect Alex Jordan built the House on the Rock.

Yikes! That sea monster is longer than the Statue of Liberty is tall!

Frank Lloyd Wright (1867–1959) was America's greatest architect. He was born in Richland Center. His home, Taliesin, is in Spring Green.

LAKE SUPERIOR

MICHIGAN

MINNESOTA

IOWA

Richland Center

Spring Green

MICHIGAN

LAKE MICHIGAN

The House on the Rock in Spring Green

You're hanging out over the valley. Look down past your feet to the forest floor. It's more than fifteen stories down! Suddenly everything begins to sway. Help!

You're in the House on the Rock in Spring Green. It's perched atop a rock tower. And you've walked into the Infinity Room. This long, pointy room sticks out in mid-air. When people walk around in the room, it moves!

This whole house is full of strange things. Just check it out. Thirty-five music machines with moving figures. More than 250 dollhouses. The world's largest carousel, with 269 carousel animals. Three giant organs, one with fifteen keyboards. And a sea monster battling a giant squid. Help!

What a view! The House on the Rock overlooks Wyoming Valley.

The Infinity Room's walls are made of 3,264 windows.

Oh, boy! Let's take the helicopter ride!

AirVenture in Oshkosh

You're soaring over Oshkosh. Your helicopter dips, swoops, and hovers. And way down there are thousands of aircraft.

You're at AirVenture! It's a big summertime aircraft festival in Oshkosh. You'll see warplanes, seaplanes, and antique planes. Even planes that people built themselves. The air shows are awesome, too. Fearless **daredevils** do amazing stunts in the air.

While you're there, stroll over to Pioneer Airport. Then hop aboard for your helicopter ride!

Careful! A skilled daredevil walks on an airplane wing at AirVenture.

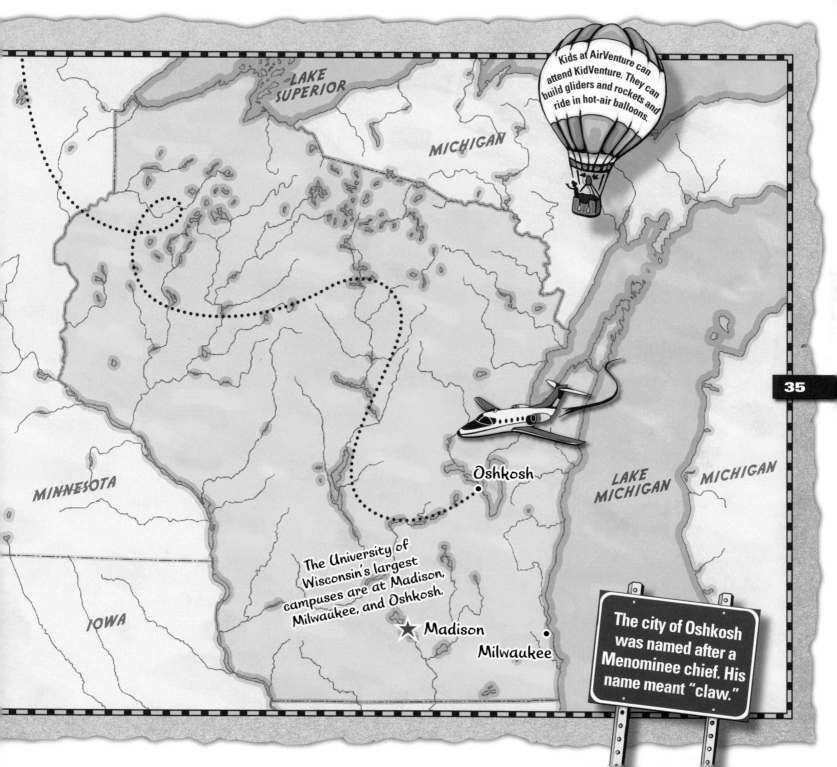

LAKE SUPERIOR

MICHIGAN

Kids at AirVenture can attend KidVenture. They can build gliders and rockets and ride in hot-air balloons.

Oshkosh

LAKE MICHIGAN

MICHIGAN

MINNESOTA

The University of Wisconsin's largest campuses are at Madison, Milwaukee, and Oshkosh.

IOWA

★ Madison

Milwaukee

The city of Oshkosh was named after a Menominee chief. His name meant "claw."

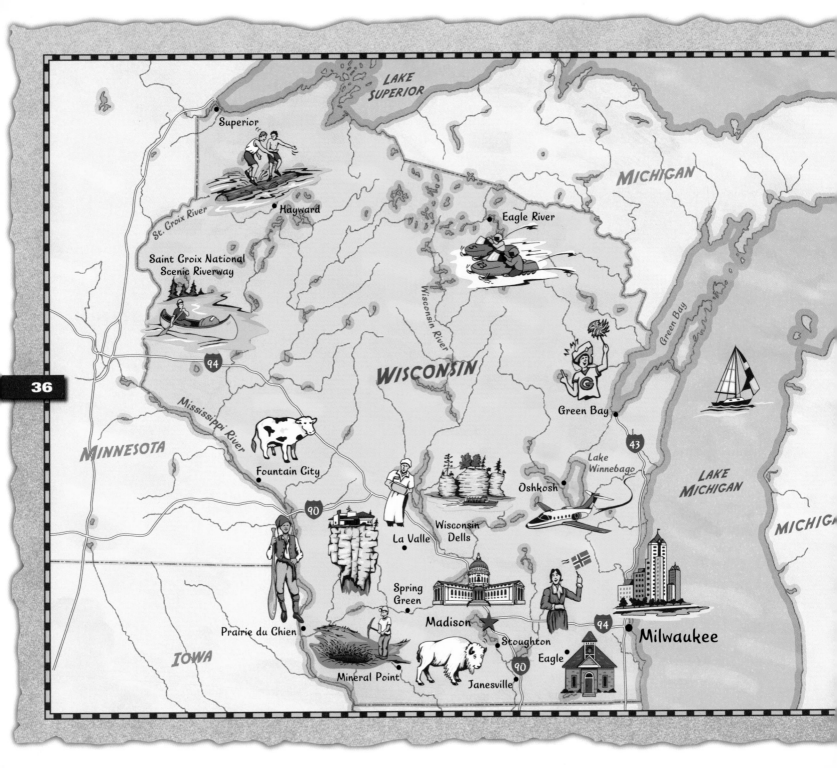

LAKE SUPERIOR

Superior

Hayward

St. Croix River

Saint Croix National Scenic Riverway

Eagle River

MICHIGAN

Wisconsin River

WISCONSIN

Green Bay

MINNESOTA

Mississippi River

Fountain City

Lake Winnebago

Oshkosh

LAKE MICHIGAN

MICHIGAN

Wisconsin Dells

La Valle

Prairie du Chien

Spring Green

Madison

Stoughton

Milwaukee

IOWA

Mineral Point

Janesville

Eagle

OUR TRIP

We visited many amazing places on our trip! We also met a lot of interesting people along the way. Look at the map on the left. Use your finger to trace all the places we have been.

What is Shake Rag Street a reminder of? See page 8 for the answer.

How high can a champion climber climb? Page 15 has the answer.

Where is the world's largest music festival held? See page 16 for the answer.

What is Rhinelander's official animal? Look on page 22 for the answer.

Where did the Republican Party get its start? Page 24 has the answer.

How many different kinds of mustard can you find in Mount Horeb? Turn to page 26 for the answer.

Who is the Packers' star quarterback? Look on page 31 and find out!

What famous architect had a home in Spring Green? Turn to page 32 for the answer.

That was a great trip! We have traveled all over Wisconsin!

There are a few places that we didn't have time for, though. Next time, we'll stop by Saint Croix National Scenic Riverway in Saint Croix Falls. People who visit canoe, hike, or fish. If they're lucky, they sometimes spot eagles, wolves, or deer!

More Places to Visit in Wisconsin

WORDS TO KNOW

architect (AR-ki-tekt) a person who designs buildings

breweries (BROO-ur-eez) places where beer is made

dairy (DAIR-ee) having to do with milk and milk products

daredevils (DAIR-dev-ilz) people who perform dangerous acts

ethnic (ETH-nik) having to do with a person's race or nationality

immigrants (IM-uh-gruhnts) people who leave their home country for another country

industry (IN-duh-stree) a type of business

legislature (LEJ-iss-lay-chur) a group of people who make laws for a state or country

lumberjacks (LUHM-bur-jaks) workers who cut down forest trees and transport them

peninsula (puh-NIN-suh-luh) a piece of land almost completely surrounded by water

tomahawk (TOM-uh-hawk) a Native American ax

troll (TROHL) a creepy creature in the folklore of Norway, Sweden, and Denmark

udder (UHD-ur) the part of a cow that holds its milk

Wisconsin covers 54,310 square miles (140,663 sq km). It's the 25th-largest state in size.

STATE SYMBOLS

State animal: Badger
State beverage: Milk
State bird: Robin
State dance: Polka
State dog: American water spaniel
State domesticated animal: Dairy cow
State fish: Muskellunge
State flower: Wood violet
State fossil: Trilobite
State grain: Corn
State insect: Honeybee
State mineral: Galena
State peace symbol: Mourning dove
State rock: Red granite
State soil: Antigo silt loam
State tree: Sugar maple
State wildlife animal: White-tailed deer

State flag

State seal

STATE SONG

"On, Wisconsin!"

Words by J. S. Hubbard and Charles D. Rosa, music by William T. Purdy

On, Wisconsin! On, Wisconsin!
Grand old badger state!
We, thy loyal sons and daughters,
Hail thee, good and great.
On, Wisconsin! On, Wisconsin!
Champion of the right,
"Forward," our motto—
God will give thee might!

FAMOUS PEOPLE

Catt, Carrie (1859–1947), women's rights activist

Ehlert, Lois (1934–), children's author and illustrator

Favre, Brett (1969–), football player

Henkes, Kevin (1960–), children's author and illustrator

Houdini, Harry (1874–1926), magician

King, Pee Wee (1914–2000), country music singer and composer

La Follette, Robert (1855–1925), governor and senator

Liberace (1919–1987), musician, entertainer

Lombardi, Vince (1913–1970), football coach

MacArthur, Douglas (1880–1964), military general

Meir, Golda (1898–1978), prime minister of Israel

Muir, John (1838–1914), naturalist, conservationist

O'Keeffe, Georgia (1887–1986), artist

Paul, Les (1915–), musician and guitar innovator

Rehnquist, William (1924–), Supreme Court chief justice

Tracy, Spencer (1900–1967), actor

Welles, Orson (1915–1985), film director, actor

Wilder, Laura Ingalls (1867–1957), author

Wilder, Thornton (1897–1975), author and playwright

Wright, Frank Lloyd (1867–1959), architect

TO FIND OUT MORE

At the Library

Lakin, Patricia. *Harry Houdini: Escape Artist*. New York: Aladdin Paperbacks, 2002.

Mara, Wil. *John Muir*. New York: Children's Press, 2002.

Wargin, Kathy-Jo, and Renee Graef (illustrator). *B Is for Badger: A Wisconsin Alphabet*. Chelsea, Mich.: Sleeping Bear Press, 2004.

Wilkes, Maria D., and Dan Andreasen (illustrator). *Little House in Brookfield*. New York: HarperCollins Publishers, 1996.

On the Web

Visit our home page for lots of links about Wisconsin:
http://www.childsworld.com/links

Note to Parents, Teachers, and Librarians: We routinely verify our Web links to make sure they are safe, active sites—so encourage your readers to check them out!

Places to Visit or Contact

Wisconsin Department of Tourism
201 W. Washington Avenue
PO Box 8690
Madison, WI 53708-8690
800/432-8747
For more information about traveling in Wisconsin

The Wisconsin Historical Museum
30 N. Carroll Street
Madison, WI 53703
608/264-6555
For more information about the history of Wisconsin

INDEX

Bye, Badger State.
We had a great time.
We'll come back soon!